Sports and Relationship Building

By

Dr. Tekemia Dorsey

Table of Contents

Chapter 1:
Introduction to Sport and Relationship

Social contacts are among the basic human needs. When the needs for health, food and security are satisfied, human beings, as social beings, develop a desire for human contact. Only then are self-realization and personality development really possible.

The desire for social contacts at work or in the family is not always sufficiently fulfilled. That's why people look for hobbies and leisure activities to meet like-minded people and just socialize. Sporting activities and the gym are ideal and are perfect for building social contacts and cultivating a common interest, namely the desire for activity and exercise.

1

Social contacts have an influence on our well-being and even contribute to leading a long and happy life. Because our aging process depends not only on age itself and some biological influencing factors, but also heavily on our personal environment (more sport and exercise in old age). It is not for nothing that the saying goes "You are as old as you feel."

The social contact with young and active people promotes our well-being and helps us to feel meaningful as well as having more energy. Social contacts thus ensure greater satisfaction and help to reduce stress factors. We just feel more balanced.

People who are alone a lot start to brood and lose touch with society. The feeling of being supported by others is an important cornerstone for feeling safe. Incidentally, society also reduces the risk of becoming depressed. Social contacts are stimulating, because the brain cells are activated in conversations and exchanges.

This also reduces the risk of becoming forgetful or developing Alzheimer's disease. It also reduces the risk of having a stroke. The reason for this is the increased performance and the feeling of being needed by others. Thus, social contacts are not only a contribution to a meaningful life, but they clearly increase life expectancy.

Social contacts are very important for humans, because we are a social being. If such contacts are missing, then we feel uncomfortable and no longer needed. Being alone is important from time to time. But real loneliness makes you sick in the long run.

Social contacts arise in the interaction between people. Through conversations, joint activities and spending time together, people exchange ideas. This exchange is for learning, for fun, but also for socialization. This is where the frames of reference are formed that makes it possible to reflect on one's own actions and communication.

Social contacts include family, friends and colleagues - but also all other encounters and interactions with people, such as in leisure time or during sports.

Social contacts are important for the various phases of socialization because they convey value systems and offer orientation to systems. They promote cultures and contribute to fair and functioning coexistence. In addition, interpersonal relationships contribute to a better attitude towards life and strengthen both physical health and the psyche, as they have a positive influence on us.

Why do social contacts prolong life? They have a calming effect on us. Because they give us a sense of belonging and let us know that there are people we can trust and who are there for us. Thus, these positive contacts help us to be more relaxed and not afraid to be alone.

They also stimulate our creativity and ensure that we think faster and more efficiently because they reconnect the synapses in our brain over and over again.

Finally, social contacts also contribute to informal learning throughout life. This promotes our solution orientation and strengthens the positive feeling, which in turn has a beneficial effect on our health. Not only friendships are there to stay mentally fit. Sport and fitness also help to increase physical activity and gain access to other people and opinions through shared hobbies.

Building Positive Social Contacts

Interpersonal relationships are not always free of conflict. The more positive social contacts we have, the more robust and secure we become in dealing with less good social contacts and can process experiences more easily. When it comes to social contacts, it is important that the quality is right. As with most things, the rule applies: less is more.

It is not the amount of social contact that shows how good or how popular we are. It is much more important that the contacts are pleasant and become our source of energy and strength.

They should enrich life and best of all, the time together is fun. Sport and leisure activities are therefore also good door openers to establish social contacts, since common interests are already emerging here.

Because what connects and strengthens us are similarities! The more we identify with the other person and share their worldview, the more positive the effect of these social contacts on body and mind.

Extroverts find it easier to approach and connect with others. But not only the willingness and personality decide whether and how we make social contacts. The experiences we made earlier in our lives in kindergarten, school, and family and work also have an influence on whether we can approach others more quickly or more slowly later in life.

The more positive experiences a person has, the easier and less self-conscious he approaches others. It can often be observed that people who were in clubs early on or who had positive and open access to others at school come into contact with others more quickly. The influence of the family and the values conveyed thereby also play a major role.

Those who play more alone in childhood and grow up as an only child often find it more difficult to make new contacts later in life. A move, a new environment or a different job also means repositioning yourself socially and establishing the necessary contacts.

Fortunately, thanks to digitization and new media, it has become easier to maintain contact with people from earlier periods of life and to continue to cultivate them.

However, the contacts in the digital world are not sufficient. We recommend leisure activities such as fitness and sports, where you can easily get to know like-minded people. Nothing is more effective for connecting than finding environments where you feel comfortable and finding people who share similar values.

Significance of Social Contacts in the Individual Phases of Socialization

A baby initially has social contact with its parents, siblings and grandparents. After that, social contacts begin outside of the direct reference persons, such as in kindergarten. Here, small children learn to assert themselves and to learn how to deal with one another. It is only in elementary school that the first conflicts and interests that need to be enforced usually come into play. Adaptation and the independent selection of friends play an important role here and thus the character is consolidated.

Social contacts enrich our lives because we find role models and orientation here. For this reason it is even dangerous to live in seclusion as an adult. Humans are living beings that live in systems and society and draw from them the mental strength to master and enjoy their lives because the other people form a framework for orientation. In exchange, one often finds one's own problems not so bad and can reduce stress through the interaction and learn to let go.

It doesn't matter whether we are children or seniors; the social contacts give us motivation and drive, as things become more binding for us. We will be active in every respect. We are valued for this and receive recognition, which in turn strengthens and builds up our own ego. An energy is created that can be shared with others.

Why Fitness and Sports Enthusiasts Find New Contacts Faster

Many find it difficult to establish social contacts. While people with children usually quickly make new contacts through them, others find it difficult at first. The fear of being rejected or even being intrusive inhibits us and our courage to approach others.

It is therefore helpful to look for a personal area of interest and to establish contacts with like-minded people. A walk together (Does walking count as exercise?), regular exercise or other hobbies can help to socialize. Visiting clubs or the gym also offers opportunities to get to know others.

On the training area or in courses, you quickly get into conversation and on club days you quickly get to know new, exciting people with whom you can find a topic of conversation right away. Often one thing quickly leads to the other.

Team sports are a gold fountain for social contacts. But individual sports and communities also offer opportunities to exchange ideas. Meetings, competitions or excursions then offer more than enough opportunities to make contacts or to maintain and strengthen existing acquaintances.

Barriers to Social Contact

Negative emotions and feelings such as envy or resentment make it difficult to establish social contacts and can lead to conflicts. Good communication and a value-free approach help to reduce these inhibitions. Social contacts are not linked to performance and should always be seen as a source of energy and as valuable time spent together.

Hierarchies are also an obstacle when it comes to establishing new contacts. That's why it's advisable to make new contacts while doing sports. It's not about performance; it's more about activating and motivating each other to do the sport instead of lying on the sofa at home.

Due to its fixed training times, sport in a club offers a framework that has something binding about it. Absences are then immediately recognized by colleagues and often addressed. So there is a certain compulsion.

If this compulsion does not limit or is even considered annoying, then this can be a positive thing. This motivates and creates more togetherness because social contacts should primarily be perceived as positive and pleasant. They are characterized by give and take and everyone involved should be on an equal footing with one another.

Approaching Others Positively

Sport releases positive emotions and is good for body and mind. This creates an important basis for why sport is very valuable as a leisure activity. If social, positive contacts result from this positive basic idea, this is perfect for promoting and expanding them.

Regular sport thus stimulates creativity and exchange, and you learn a wide variety of things from other people. This can bring generations together, but also lead to a fruitful exchange in mutual cooperation, where you give what you can give and take what you are offered.

It makes the world a little better and provides more balance and a good body feeling and mental balance. The worries are reduced, tensions subside and you can just let yourself go in a good and familiar atmosphere and let the others catch you, because social contacts are there for that too!

And what could be better than having a healthy body coupled with a healthy mind and friends who are there for you when you need them. This strengthens our sense of security and lets us live longer and healthier!

Chapter 2:
Sport as a Social "Integrator"

Integration is the set of social and cultural processes that make the individual a member of a society. It seems obvious but, especially nowadays, it is not so simple to implement. We live in a world that by its nature or rather by the nature of the individuals that compose it, tends not to put us on the same level, and to label us based on our history, cultural background, our problems of a personal nature.

Since the 1950s, the best channels have been studied for transmitting the values of equality, solidarity and cooperation to society. The encounter between different cultures and the enhancement of the resulting differences are fundamental themes for the construction of a just, respectful, and globalized world.

What could be the answer to an ever increasing demand for organization, inclusion and social integration? The answers are multiple, of course. But many of these revolve around our favorite word "sport".

Sport as a Tool for Social Integration

The development of today's society cannot ignore putting sporting activity at the center of a process of social synergy. But the question that arises is: sport, why? Sport, it goes without saying, conveys some life lessons which, disguised as fun and apparently "only" physical activities, have the power to cross everyone. While the mind over the years becomes the victim of all those social and cultural constructs that often limit our judgment and make us dull, closed, and often underline the "different", the physical is still matter. A body reacts in a natural way by adapting to the context in which it is inserted, and has the power to "make us forget" all those superstructures given by prejudice and mental limits that often prevent us from including our neighbor, because apparently unpleasant.

19

Why autistic? Is it because of color or with almond-shaped eyes? Why female? Why Effeminate? That child is dressing up oddly. Or he listens to weird music. That girl is fat. She has an old-fashioned hairstyle. Maybe she thinks differently from us. Or it will be that we vote who we do not like. Well, she believes in God. Or, well, she believes in Buddha. You made a mistake. Or, she never commits any. In short, we do not notice, but we are constantly subject to give a vote to those around us.

Sports for All

But how do you stop? He is stronger than us, making judgments. But there must be a way to eliminate the differences and make them strengths. Our common point, because of all, common, because it unites every human being. It is the similar reaction to certain external stimuli, be they heat, fatigue, hunger. Everyone, if they touch a hot pan, automatically retracts their hand. Or, if they struggle, they pant. Everyone, if they are hungry, looks for food.

It is the physical sensations that make us all the same. And it is always an external stimulus that can be interpreted by everyone in the same way that, reacting in a more instinctive way, has the power to create associations of ideas and to transmit to our brain a number of values that would be almost impossible to explain in words.

Sport as Social Integration in Prisoners

The power of sport lies precisely in its implicit values, which educate and re-educate, which stimulate and transmit, which nourish and make us grow. Can sport also have the power to re-educate?

In one of the most difficult contexts to manage, the answer that scholars have given themselves has been affirmative. Sport thus becomes a tool for social inclusion even among prisoners. Prisons, nowadays, are all based on one great basic principle which is the goal of detention must not be mere penance, but re-education. Guaranteeing these people physical and motor activity then becomes one of the aspects through which to prevent the punishment from becoming" pure social retaliation ".

Detention is often the cause or consequence of a physical and mental deterioration in the person who suffers it. Sport has been identified as an active response to this problem. For this reason, Sport in prison has been created for the recovery of prisoners, in order to promote healthy sports activities that can teach self-control, respect, and discipline.

Sporting activity, having the power to release and lower tension and stress, thus also becomes a stimulus for a more peaceful coexistence within the structure. The goal is to give back to society proactive citizens who, in addition to an inner and psychic work, may have learned values such as self-esteem, team spirit and mutual help.

Sport as a Social Aggregator in Suburbs and Disadvantaged Contexts

Sports practice can also indeed, must also be understood as an educational and social tool. We have already said several times that Sport is culture. Therefore, its immense power also affects those situations of territorial difficulty that often prevent children from growing up in a favorable social context. This is why sport, and specifically the figure of the coach, becomes fundamental stimuli to be able to "detach" oneself even from degraded territorial contexts, finding in Sport a healthy, stimulating and educational environment. Furthermore, sport can be won as a great supplement for all those minorities at risk of social emancipation. In fact, sport overcomes any barrier; as they say "to play football you don't have to speak the same

24

language". To play basketball you don't need to know that

you are rich or poor or whether your skin is light or dark.

Sport as Inclusion and Teaching in Disabilities

Overcome obstacles, breaking down barriers. Sport also has this power. For this reason, the added value of sporting practice is best expressed in the social inclusion of people with psychomotor disabilities. It is neither a question of volunteering, nor of "giving everyone the same opportunities" or rather, not only. The true mission of sport, also and above all in this context, is to fight negative stereotypes, and to convey to everyone that the term incapable does not exist.

And here the Sport becomes another invaluable opportunity to learn. Sports practice and training teach the person with disabilities to value their person. Sport improves coordination, increases muscle strength, improves skills such as interpersonal communication, and causes   general   self-satisfaction.

To the person without disabilities, to observe or train alongside those who fight more than one battle every day, Sport teaches acceptance and amazement, the true and sincere amazement of those who see the magic of Sport and the beauty of human beings.

Chapter 3:
Sports Intended as a Social and Educational Tool

Sport as an Educational Tool

For children it is a game in all respects, which teaches them to listen, observe the rules, respect their peers and socialize; in adolescence, the focus shifts to the body, muscles, weight and goals to be achieved.

A real educational agency, sport is therefore synonymous with commitment and perseverance, which tests each of us, helping us to overcome limits and make dreams come true. Today there are many young people who are experiencing an identity crisis capable of triggering feelings of insecurity, vulnerability and fragility. And it is precisely in a similar context that sport, as an educational vehicle, has a central role, since it trains people as such, even before athletes.

But when it comes to education in reference to sport, we must not forget who is responsible for carrying out this mission successfully. This is how the figure of the coach becomes, therefore, central in the life of the youngest, what a good sports educator is called to do, in order to best perform his role, is to release the self-esteem of the boys from the result, to stimulate the assumption of responsibility and autonomy, to safeguard the right to make mistakes and then start over.

The coach, in fact, becomes the third fundamental figure for the growth of the child, after the parents and the school, performing at the same time the task of teacher, model, instructor and animator.

Chapter 4:
Sport as a Social Function

Nelson Mandela stated that "Sport has the power to change the world. It has the power to arouse emotions. It has the power to bring people together like few other things. It has the power to awaken hope where previously there was only despair".

In fact, one of the foundations of sport is to force children to live in a group, to then feel part of a certain social context. This, in fact, is considered by many sociologists to be one of the primary needs of each individual, without which he would not be able to live in a condition of normality and harmony with himself.

There is no doubt that sport is a vehicle for inclusion, aggregation and participation with a fundamental social role, which allows the development of skills and abilities essential for balanced growth. Whether it is for children, teenagers, adults or the elderly, it represents a school of life, which never stops teaching new rules: being with others, sharing, contributing to the achievement of difficult, challenging, but not impossible goals. .

The common sense of belonging and participation are powerful weapons, which, little by little, can bring about the change that has always been identified in sport, favoring greater economic and social cohesion, but also greater integration between the parts of society. Less represented groups, people with disabilities or from disadvantaged backgrounds. Sport, regardless of age, religion or social origin, has a great aggregative value and promotes physical and social well-being.

Virtuous Examples in Difficult Contexts

A right of all and that should not be denied to anyone, sport, as the Council of the European Union has repeatedly emphasized, is a source and engine of social inclusion, as well as a tool for the integration of minorities and groups at risk of social exclusion.

This is the reason why many sports societies and organizations promote, in a concrete way, processes of participation in sport that completely disregard people's economic, social and individual conditions.

The natural distinctions of language, color and origin are fundamental for the development of children who practice sports. In the game, in fact, there are diversity of roles and characteristics which, together, form the winning team.

Conclusion

An essential component for the psychophysical development of the human being, sport has always played a decisive role in our culture, both social and family, thanks to its educational function. The anthropologist Marcel Mauss defines sporting practice as a social fact, that is, a complex of activities that includes different areas, ranging from purely sports to politics.

Sport is the mirror of our society, capable of transmitting more or less virtuous models of life and behavioral practices. It therefore represents an important training moment, both from a motor and psychological-emotional point of view, capable of actively contributing to the formation of the personalities of the subjects involved.

Nonetheless, it is not enough to play sport to grow well for children, sporting activity must represent a moment of play and fun, without constraints or excess of expectations , which allows them to understand that life can be lost, even when there is committed to the maximum of possibilities.

With reference to our social experience, sport almost seems to represent an autonomous and distinct sphere, totally rooted in the economic and social fabric, which every day becomes an integral part of the lifestyle of all of us.

Discipline is one of the values most closely linked to sports. In fact, to face training and competitions in the best conditions, they must necessarily lead a balanced, regular life, made up of healthy habits and rest.

This is an important factor, which helps young people to get used to structuring their time, to control their character, to respect the commitment made and the times required by it.

If you approach sport correctly, therefore, you can produce well-being on several aspects health, cognitive growth, but also inclusion and respect for different cultures.

References

Duda, J.L. & Treasure, D.C. (2006). Motivational processes and the facilitation of performance, persistence, and well-being in sport. In J.M. Williams (Ed.), Applied Sport Psychology: Personal Growth to Peak Performance.

Danish, S.J.; Forneris, T.; Wallace, I. (2005). "Sport-based life skills programming in the schools". Journal of Applied School Psychology.

Vealey, R.S. (1986). "Conceptualization of sport-confidence and competitive orientation: Preliminary investigation and instrument development". Journal of Sport Psychology

Silva, J. M. (1989). "Toward the professionalization of sport psychology". The Sport Psychologist

www.ingramcontent.com/pod-product-compliance
Lightning Source LLC
Chambersburg PA
CBHW050656270326
41927CB00012B/3056